Paper

Claire Llewellyn

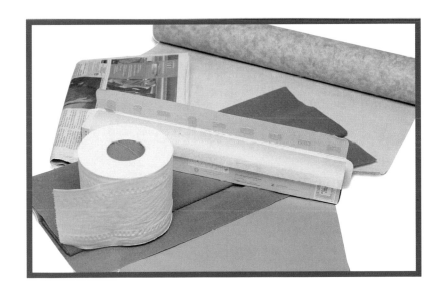

W

FRANKLIN WATTS
LONDON • SYDNEY

First published in 2004
by Franklin Watts
96 Leonard Street
London EC2A 4XD

Franklin Watts Australia
45-51 Huntley Street
Alexandria, NSW 2015

Series advisor: Gill Matthews, non-fiction literacy consultant
and Inset trainer
Editor: Rachel Cooke
Series design: Peter Scoulding
Designer: James Marks
Photography: Ray Moller unless otherwise credited
Acknowledgements: Mark Edwards/Still Pictures: 17b. Hewlett Packard: 9t. Alan Majchrowicz/Still
Pictures: 14. Sally Morgan/Ecoscene: 16, 17t. Helene Rogers/Art Directors/Trip: 13b.
Syracuse Newspapers/Image Works/Topham: 19t. J.C. Vincent/Still Pictures: 15.
Thanks to our models Jaydee Cozzi, Jakob Hawker, Hayley Sapsford and Phoebus Zavros

A CIP catalogue record for this book is available from the British Library.

ISBN: 0 7496 5721 9

Printed in Malaysia

Contents

Paper is useful

Paper is a very useful material.
It is used to make all sorts of things.

▼ *These things are all made of paper.*

Kitchen roll

Writing paper

Bank notes

4

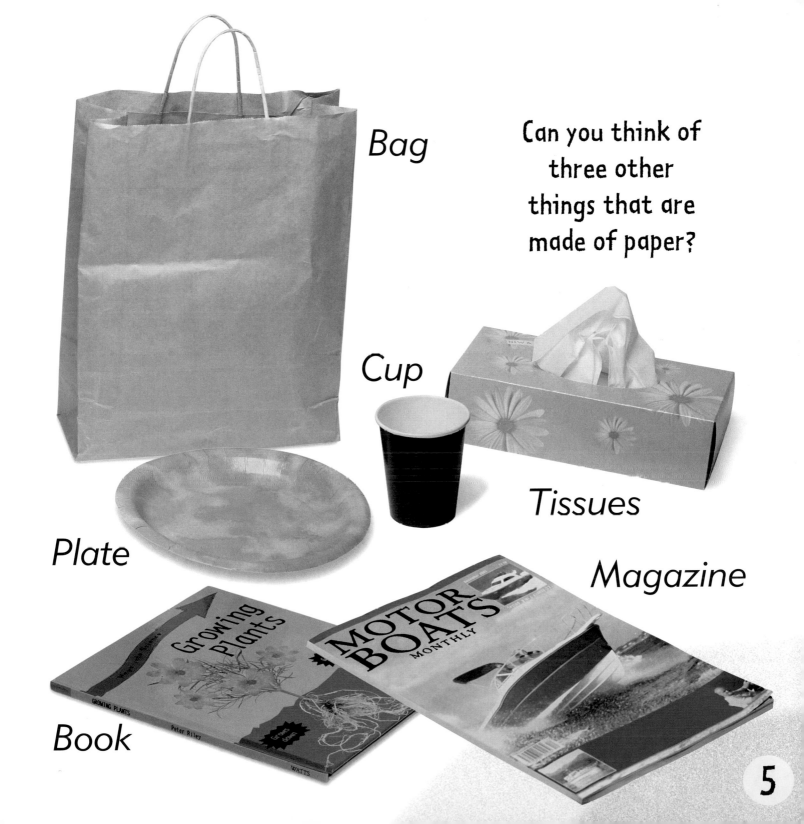

Bag

Can you think of
three other
things that are
made of paper?

Cup

Tissues

Plate

Magazine

Book

5

All kinds of paper

There are many kinds of paper.
Each one has its own look and feel.

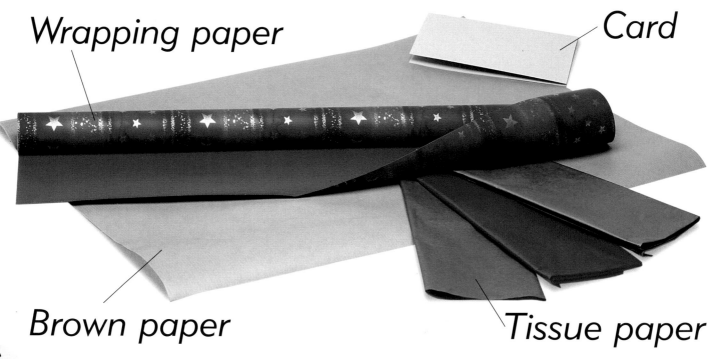

Wrapping paper

Card

Brown paper

Tissue paper

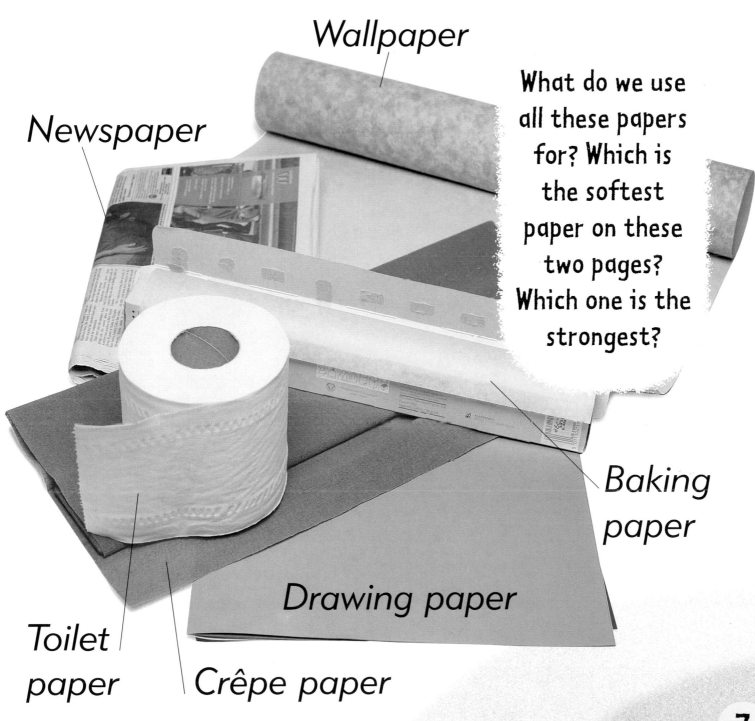

Wallpaper

Newspaper

What do we use all these papers for? Which is the softest paper on these two pages? Which one is the strongest?

Baking paper

Drawing paper

Toilet paper

Crêpe paper

We write on paper

Paper is very smooth.

► *Paper is easy to write on and paint on.*

▶ *Machines can print on paper, too.*

We cannot write on all paper. What happens when you write on soft paper with a felt-tip pen?

Paper is strong

Some paper is very strong.
We use it to pack
and protect things.

► *Some foods
are packed
in paper.*

 *A strong cardboard box is always useful.*

Some things break very easily. Soft paper helps to protect them from bumps.

Paper soaks up water

Some paper is soft and soaks up water. We use it, then throw it away.

►*We use paper tissues to blow our nose.*

We use kitchen roll to wipe up a spill.

Not all paper soaks up water. This paper cup and carton have been coated to make them waterproof.

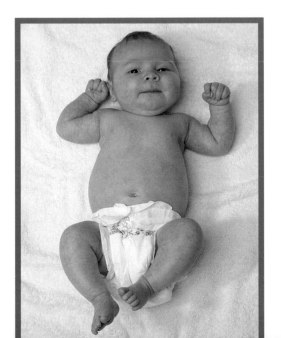

Paper nappies help to keep the baby dry!

Paper is made from wood

Paper is made from wood. Wood comes from trees.

Wood is a natural material. It is made by nature, not by people.

▲ *People grow trees for making paper in forests called plantations.*

▲ *The trees are cut into logs and taken to a paper mill.*

Making paper

At the paper mill, the logs are cut into bits. Then they are made into paper.

▶*The bits of wood are mixed with water to make a soggy pulp.*

The pulp is spread into a long, flat sheet.

Sometimes old paper is used to make new paper. This is called recycling.

The sheet is flattened. It dries into paper.

How is the paper used?

Paper from the paper mill is used in different ways.

Some paper is cut into sheets.

Look at a newspaper and this book. What is the same about the paper they are made of? What is different?

▲ *Some is used to make newspapers and books.*

◄ *Some goes to factories to make cardboard.*

Paper is easy to cut and shape

Paper is easy to work with.

▶ You can draw on it...

What things have you made out of paper?

20

fold it...

cut it...

curl it...

and stick it.

21

I know that...

1 Paper is useful.

2 There are many kinds of paper.

3 We write on paper.

4 Paper is strong.

5 Paper soaks up water.

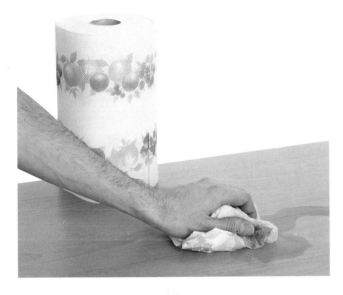

6 Paper is made from wood.

7 Paper is made at a paper mill.

8 The paper is cut up into sheets or used to make boxes, books and newspapers.

9 Paper is easy to cut and shape.

Index

About this book

I Know That! is designed to introduce children to the process of gathering information and using reference books, one of the key skills needed to begin more formal learning at school. For this reason, each book's structure reflects the information books children will use later in their learning career – with key information in the main text and additional facts and ideas in the captions. The panels give an opportunity for further activities, ideas or discussions. The contents page and index are helpful reference guides.

The language is carefully chosen to be accessible to children just beginning to read. Illustrations support the text but also give information in their own right; active consideration and discussion of images is another key referencing skill. The main aim of the series is to build confidence – showing children how much they already know and giving them the ability to gather new information for themselves. With this in mind, the *I know that...* section at the end of the book is a simple way for children to revisit what they already know as well as what they have learnt from reading the book.